THE UKULELE SONGBOOK

Thomas Balinger

VOL. II — 50 ALL TIME CLASSICS

Ukulele tuning:

Other titles by Thomas Balinger:

The Ukulele Songbook – 50 All Time Classics
The Ukulele Songbook – 50 All Time Classics, Vol. II
The Ukulele Songbook – Best of Gospel
The Ukulele Songbook – Children's Songs

Most wanted Ukulele Chords

Thomas Balinger
The Ukulele Songbook – All Time Classics – Volume 2

thomasbalinger@gmail.com

© 2014

Revised edition 2015

ISBN: 978-1505664096

Preface

I was more than a bit surprised by the warm welcome my first „Ukulele Classics" songbook was greeted with. I'd never thought there were that many Ukulele aficionados out there or that so many of you would like my book (Thanks, that means a lot to me).

Most comments on the book were really nice, with the occasional critical point made or error pointed out. There's one thing, however, everybody seemed to agree about: „Where's more?"

So here it is, fellow Ukulele players – another collection of great songs you most probably know, arranged for easy Ukulele in C (G-C-E-A). As usual, I added chord symbols, chord diagrams and melody tab to the notation to make playing these songs as easy and straightforward as possible.

The songs cover a wide range of musical styles, from „Shenandoah", "Waltzing Matilda" and „Whiskey in the jar" to „Aloa Oe" and „Banks of Sacramento" – I'm sure you'll find something you like on these pages!

If you want to accompany yourself (or others), you'll especially like the section on easy strumming and picking patterns you can use on their own or as a starting point to create your own accompaniments.

Wishing you lots of fun,

Thomas Balinger

Contents

Songs

Danny Boy

shad - ow, oh Dan - ny boy, oh Dan - ny boy, I love you so!

2. But when you come, and all the flowers are dying,
   And If I'm dead, as dead I well may be,
   You come and find the place where I am lying,
   And kneel and say an Ave there for me;

3. And I shall hear, though soft you tread above me,
   And all my grave will warmer, sweeter be,
   For you will bend and tell me that you love me,
   And I shall sleep in peace until you come to me!

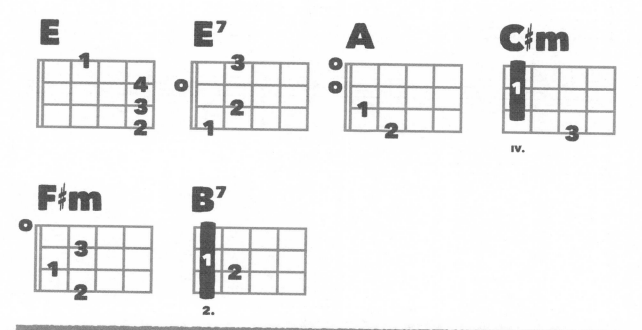

Banks of Allan Water

2. On the banks of Allan Water,
   When brown autumn spread his store.
   There I saw the miller's daughter,
   But she smiled no more.
   For the summer, grief had brought her
   And the soldier false was he,
   On the banks of Allan Water,
   None so sad as she.

3. On the banks of Allan Water,
   When the winter snow fell fast.
   Still was seen the miller's daughter
   Chilling blew the blast.
   But the miller's lovely daughter,
   Both from cold and care was free.
   On the banks of Allan Water
   There a corpse lay she.

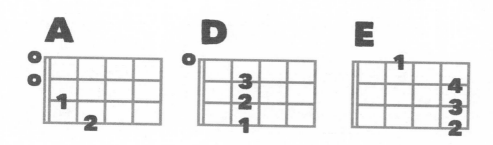

Home! Sweet Home!

Home! Sweet Home!

2. *An exile from home, spendor dazzles in vain,*
   Oh, give me my lowly thatched cottage again;
   The birds singing gaily, that come at my call;
   Give me them, with that peace of mind, dearer than all.

3. *To thee, I'll return, overburdened with care,*
   The heart's dearest solace will smile on me there.
   No more from that cottage again will I roam,
   Be it ever so humble, there's no place like home.

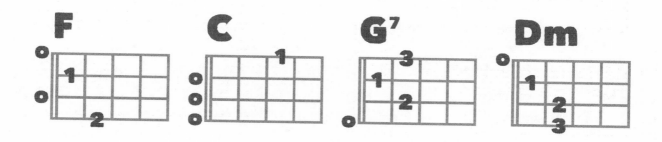

It's a long way to Tipperary

It's a long way to Tipperary

Good - bye   Pic - ca - dil - ly,   Fare - well,   Leices - ter

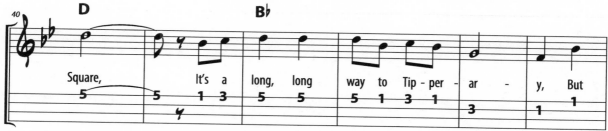

Square,   It's a   long,   long   way to Tip - per - ar - y,   But

my   hear's   right   there!"   "It's a   there!"

2. Paddy wrote a letter
   To his Irish Molly-O,
   Saying, „Should you not receive it,
   Write and let me know!"
   „If I make mistakes in spelling,
   Molly, dear," said he,
   „Remember, it's the pen that's bad,
   Don't lay the blame on me!

3. Molly wrote a neat reply
   To Irish Paddy-O,
   Saying „Mike Maloney
   Wants to marry me, and so
   Leave the Strand and Piccadilly
   Or you'll be to blame,
   For love has fairly drove me silly:
   Hoping you're the same!"

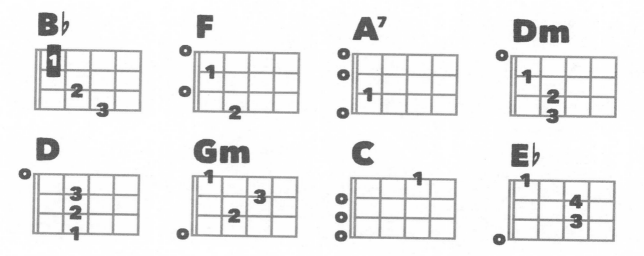

Aloha Oe

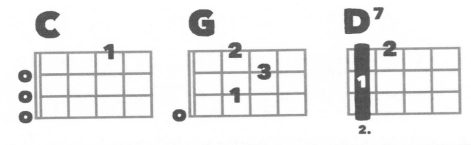

Old black Joe

2. *Why do I weep when my heart should feel no pain?*
   Why do I sigh that my friends come not again?
   Grieving for forms now departed long ago,
   I hear their gentle voices calling, "Old Black Joe."

3. *Where are the hearts once so happy and so free?*
   The children so dear that I held upon my knee?
   Gone to the shore where my soul has longed to go,
   I hear their gentle voices calling, "Old Black Joe."

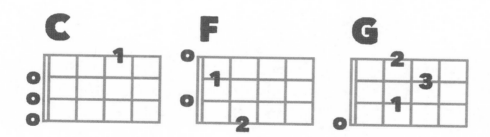

Waltzing Matilda

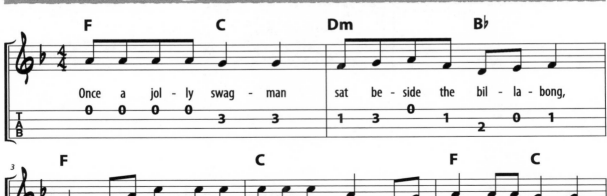

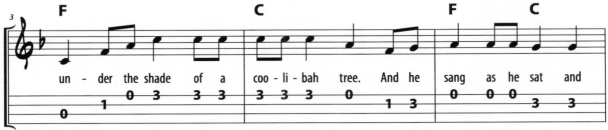

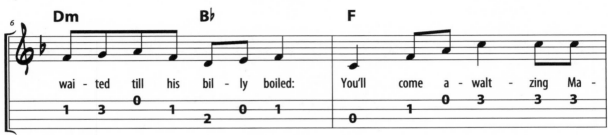

2. Down came a jumbuck to drink at that billabong.
   Up jumped the swagman and grabbed him with glee.
   And he sang as he shoved that jumbuck in his tucker bag:
   „You'll come a-waltzing Matilda, with me."
   Waltzing Matilda, waltzing Matilda
   „You'll come a-waltzing Matilda, with me",
   And he sang as he shoved that jumbuck in his tucker bag:
   „You'll come a-waltzing Matilda, with me."

3. Up rode the squatter, mounted on his thoroughbred.
   Down came the troopers, one, two, and three.
   „Whose is that jumbuck you've got in your tucker bag?
   You'll come a-waltzing Matilda, with me."
   Waltzing Matilda, waltzing Matilda
   „You'll come a-waltzing Matilda, with me",
   „Whose is that jumbuck you've got in your tucker bag?
   You'll come a-waltzing Matilda, with me."

4. Up jumped the swagman and sprang into the billabong.
   „You'll never take me alive!" said he
   And his ghost may be heard as you pass by that billabong:
   „Who'll come a-waltzing Matilda, with me?"
   Waltzing Matilda, waltzing Matilda
   „You'll come a-waltzing Matilda, with me",
   And his ghost may be heard as you pass by that billabong:
   „Who'll come a-waltzing Matilda, with me?"

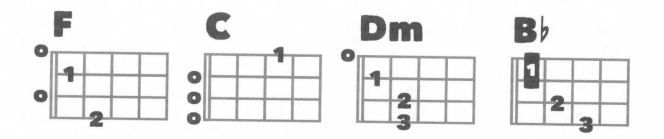

Turkey in the straw

2. Went out to milk and I didn't know how
   I milked the goat instead of the cow.
   A monkey sittin' on a pile of straw
   A winkin' at his mother-in-law.

3. I came to the river and I couldn't get across,
   So I paid five dollars for a big bay hoss.
   Well, he wouldn't go ahead and he wouldn't stand still,
   So he went up and down like an old saw mill.

4. Did you ever go fishin' on a warm summer day,
   When all the fish were swimmin' in the bay.
   With their hands in their pockets and their pockets in their pants.
   Did you ever see a fishie do the Hootchy-Kootchy Dance?

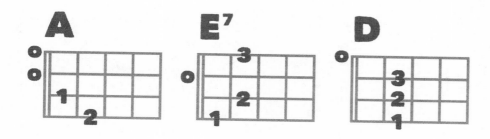

Whiskey in the jar

2. I counted out his money, and it made a pretty penny.
I put it in my pocket and I took it home to Jenny.
She said and she swore, that she never would deceive me,
but the devil take the women, for they never can be easy.

3. I went into my chamber, all for to take a slumber,
I dreamt of gold and jewels and for sure it was no wonder.
But Jenny took my charges and she filled them up with water,
Then sent for captain Farrel to be ready for the slaughter.

4. It was early in the morning, as I rose up for travel,
The guards were all around me and likewise captain Farrel.
I first produced my pistol, for she stole away my rapier,
But I couldn't shoot the water so a prisoner I was taken.

5. If anyone can aid me, it's my brother in the army,
If I can find his station down in Cork or in Killarney.
And if he'll come and save me, we'll go roving near Kilkenny,
And I swear he'll treat me better than me darling sportling Jenny.

6. Now some men take delight in the drinking and the roving,
But others take delight in the gambling and the smoking.
But I take delight in the juice of the barley,
And courting pretty fair maids in the morning bright and early.

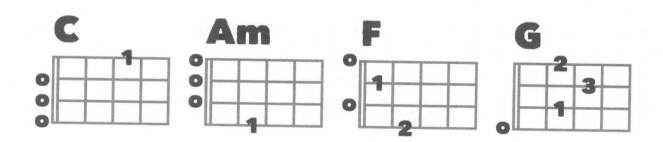

Shalom chaverim

Sha - lom chav - er - rim, sha - lom chav - er - im, sha -

lom, sha - lom. Till we meet a - gain, till we

meet a - gain. Sha - lom, sha - lom.

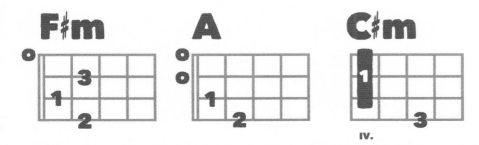

F#m   A   C#m

IV.

Banks of Sacramento

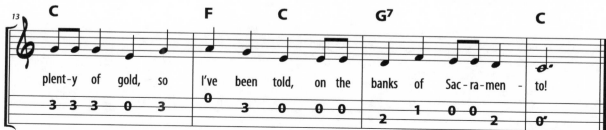

2. Oh, heave, my lads, oh heave and sing,
   Oh, heave and make those oak sticks sing.
3. Our money gone, we shipped to go,
   Around Cape Horn, through ice and snow.
4. Oh, around the Horn with a mainskys'l set
   Around Cape Horn and we're all wringin' wet.

5. Around Cape Horn in the month of May,
   With storm winds blowing every day.
6. It was in the year eighteen forty-nine,
   It was in the year eighteen forty-nine.

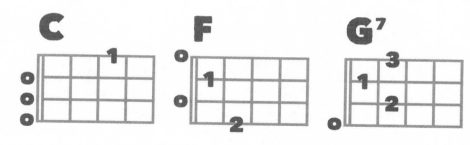

Bound for the Rio Grande

2. So it's pack up your sea-chest an' get underway,
   The girls we are leavin' can have our half-pay.

3. Our ship went sailin' over the bar,
   We've pointed her bow to the southern stars.

4. You Liverpool judies, we'll have you to know,
   We're bound to the south'ard and glad for to go.

5. We're a Liverpool ship and a Liverpool crew,
   You can stick to the coast but I'm damned if we do!

6. Goodbye to Ellen and Molly and Sue,
   You park lane judies, it's goodbye to you.

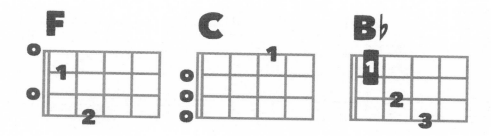

Bill Bailey

2. On one summer's day, the sun was shining fine.
   The lady love of old Bill Bailey was hanging clothes on the line
   In her back yard, and weeping hard.
   She married a B & O brakeman that took and throw'd her down.
   Bellering like a prune-fed calf with a big gang hanging ,round;
   And to that crowd she yelled out loud.

3. Bill drove by that door in an automobile,
   A great big diamond coach and footman, hear that big wench squeal;
   „He's all alone," I heard her groan.
   She hollered through that door, „Bill Bailey is you sore?
   Stop a minute; won't you listen to me? Won't I see you no more?"
   Bill winked his eye, as he heard her cry.

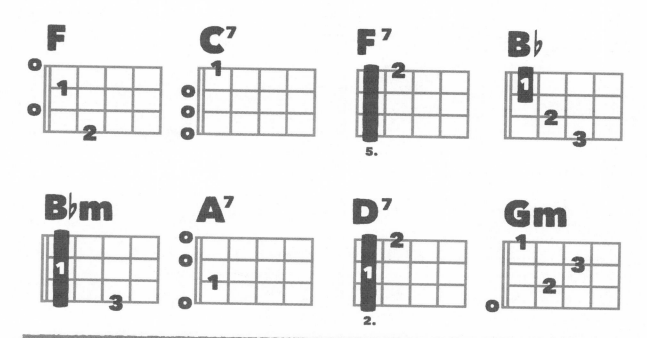

The ballad of John Henry

2. The captain said to John Henry:
   „Gonna bring that steam drill 'round,
   Gonna bring that sterm drill out on the job,
   Gonna whop that steel on down, Lord, Lord,
   Gonna whop that steel on down."

3. John Henry told his captain:
   „A man ain't nothing but a man,
   But before I let your steam drill beat me down,
   I'd die with a hammer in my hand, Lord, Lord,
   I'd die with a hammer in my hand."

4. John Henry said to his shaker:
   „Shaker, why don't you sing?
   I'm throwin' thirty pounds from my hips on down,
   Just listen to that cold steel ring, Lord, Lord,
   Just listen to that cold steel ring."

5. John Henry said to his shaker:
   „Shaker, you'd better pray,
   'Cause if I miss that little piece of steel,
   Tomorrow be your buryin' day, Lord, Lord,
   Tomorrow be your buryin' day."

6. The shaker said to John Henry:
   „I think this mountain's cavin' in!"
   John Henry said to his shaker, „Man,
   That ain't nothin' but my hammer suckin' wind! Lord, Lord,
   That ain't nothin' but my hammer suckin' wind!"

7. Now the man that invented the steam drill,
   Thought he was mighty fine.
   But John Henry made fifteen feet,
   The steam drill only made nine, Lord, Lord,
   The steam drill only made nine.

8. John Henry hammered in the mountains,
   His hammer was striking fire.
   But he worked so hard, he broke his poor heart,
   He laid down his hammer and he died, Lord, Lord,
   He laid down his hammer and he died.

9. John Henry had a little woman,
   Her name was Polly Ann.
   John Henry took sick and went to his bed,
   Polly Ann drove steel like a man, Lord, Lord,
   Polly Ann drove steel like a man.

10. John Henry had a little baby,
    You could hold him in the palm of your hand.
    The last words I heard that poor boy say:
    „My daddy was a steel driving man, Lord, Lord,
    My daddy was a steel driving man."

11. They took John Henry to the graveyard,
    And they buried him in the sand.
    And every locomotive comes a-roaring by
    Says „There lies a steel-driving man, Lord, Lord,
    There lies a steel-driving man."

12. Well every Monday morning,
    When the bluebirds begin to sing,
    You can hear John Henry a mile or more,
    You can hear John Henry's hammer ring, Lord, Lord,
    You can hear John Henry's hammer ring.

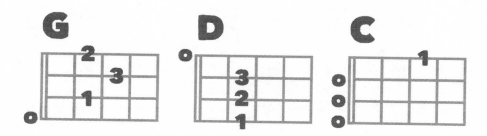

The Wabash Cannon Ball

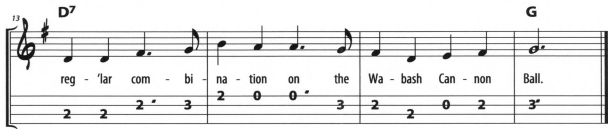

Chorus:
Listen to the jingle, the rumble and the roar
as she glides along the woodland, through the hills and by the shore.
Hear the mighty rush of the engine, hear that lonesome hobo squall.
You're travelling through the jungles on the Wabash Cannonball.

2. *She came down from Birmingham, one cold December day*
   As she rolled into the station, you could hear all the people say,
   "There's a girl from Tennessee, she's long and she's tall
   She came down from Birmingham on the Wabash Cannonball."

3. *Our the Eastern states are dandy so the people always say,*
   "From New York to St. Louis and Chicago by the way
   From the hills of Minnesota where the rippling waters fall,
   No changes can be taken on that Wabash Cannonball."

4. *Here's to daddy Claxton, may his name forever stand*
   And always be remembered 'round the courts of Alabam'.
   His earthly race is over and the curtains 'round him fall.
   We'll carry him home to victory on the Wabash Cannonball.

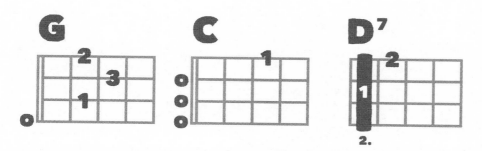

Old folks at home

2. All 'round the little farm I wandered,
   When I was young
   Then many happy days I squandered,
   Many the songs I sung
   When I was playing with my brother,
   Happy was I
   Oh, take me to my kind old mother,
   There let me live and die.

3. One little hut among the bushes,
   One that I love
   Still sadly to my mem'ry rushes,
   No matter where I rove
   When shall I see the bees a-humming,
   All 'round the comb
   When shall I hear the banjo strumming,
   Down by my good old home.

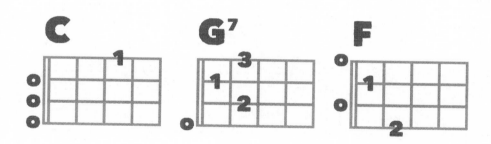

The coast of High Barbaree

There were two lof - ty ships from old Eng - land came, Blow high! Blow low! And so sailed we, one was the Prince o' Lu - ther an' the oth - er Prince 'o Wales, all a - cruis - in down the coasts of the High Barb - a - ree!

The coast of High Barbaree

2. „Look ahead, look astern,
Look a-weather and a-lee,"
Blow high, blow low,
and so say we;
„Aloft there at the masthead
Just see what you can see,"
Cruising down along the coast
Of the High Barbaree.

3. „There's nought upon the stern,
There's nought upon the lee,"
Blow high, blow low, and so say we;
„But there's a lofty ship to windward
And she's sailing fast and free,"
Cruising down along the coast
Of the High Barbaree.

4. „O hail her! O hail her!"
Our gallant Captain cried,
Blow high, blow low,
and so say we;
„Are you a man-o-war
Or a privateer?" said he,
Cruising down along the coast
Of the High Barbaree.

5. „O I am not a man-o-war
Nor privateer," said he;
Blow high, blow low,
and so say we;
„But I'm a salt-sea pirate
Whose a-looking for his fee,"
Cruising down along the coast
Of the High Barbaree.

6. O 'twas broadside to broadside
A long time lay we,
Blow high, blow low,
and so say we;
Until we shot her masts away
And blew them in the sea,
Cruising down along the coast
Of the High Barbaree.

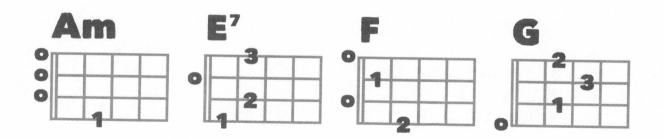

Whiskey Johnny

2. Whiskey here, whiskey there,
   Whiskey almost everywhere.

3. Whiskey up and whiskey down,
   Whiskey all around the town.

4. Whiskey killed me poor old dad,
   Whiskey drove me mother mad.

5. My wife and I do not agree.
   She puts whiskey in her tea.

6. I had a girl and her name was Lize.
   She puts whiskey in her pies.

7. Oh whiskey straight, and whiskey strong,
   Give me some whiskey and I'll sing you a song.

8. If whiskey comes too near my nose,
   I tip it up and down she goes.

9. Some likes whiskey, some likes beer,
   I wisht I had a barrel here.

10. Whiskey made me pawn me clothes.
    Whiskey gave me this broken nose.

11. Oh the mate likes whiskey, the skipper likes rum.
    The sailors like both but me can't get none.

12. Whiskey is the life of man,
    Whiskey from that old tin can.

13. I thought I heard the first mate say,
    I treats me crew in a decent way.

14. If whiskey was a river and I could swim,
    I'd say here goes and dive right in.

15. If whiskey was a river and I was a duck,
    I'd dive to the bottom and never come up.

16. I wisht I knew where whiskey grew,
    I'd eat the leaves and the branches too.

17. A tot of whiskey all around
    And a bottle full for the shanty man.

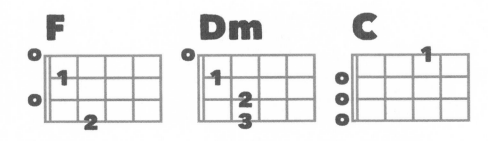

Down in the valley

2. Roses love sunshine, violets love dew,
Angels in Heaven know I love you,
Know I love you, dear, know I love you,
Angels in Heaven know I love you.

3. If you don't love me, love whom you please,
Throw your arms round me, give my heart ease,
Give my heart ease, dear, give my heart ease,
Throw your arms round me, give my heart ease

4. Build me a castle, forty feet high;
So I can see her as she rides by,
As she rides by, dear, as she rides by,
So I can see her as she rides by.

5. Write me a letter, send it by mail;
Send it in care of the Birmingham jail,
Birmingham jail, dear, Birmingham jail,
Send it in care of the Birmingham jail.

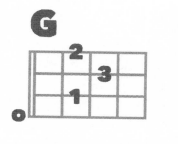

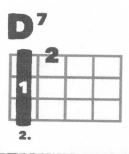

Will the circle be unbroken

2. I said to the undertaker,
   "Undertaker please drive slow.
   For that body you are carrying,
   Lord, I hate to see her go."

3. Well I followed close behind her,
   Tried to hold up and be brave.
   But I could not hide my sorrow,
   When they laid her in that grave.

4. I went back home, Lord, that home was lonesome.
   Since my mother, she was gone,
   All my brothers and sisters crying.
   What a home so sad and alone.

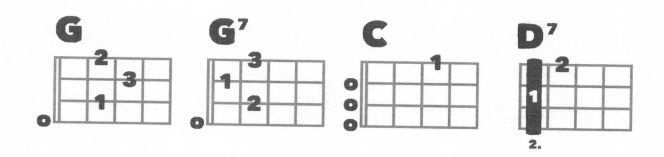

The last rose of summer

The last rose of summer

2. I'll not leave thee, thou lone one!
   To pine on the stem;
   Since the lovely are sleeping,
   Go, sleep thou with them.
   Thus kindly I scatter,
   Thy leaves o'er the bed,
   Where thy mates of the garden
   Lie scentless and dead.

3. So soon may I follow,
   When friendships decay,
   And from Love's shining circle
   The gems drop away.
   When true hearts lie withered,
   And fond ones are flown,
   Oh! who would inhabit
   This bleak world alone?

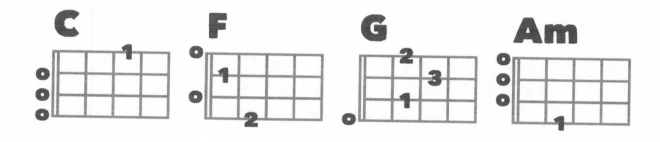

Red river valley

From this val - ley they say you are go-ing, we will miss your bright

eyes and sweet smile, for they say you are tak - ing the

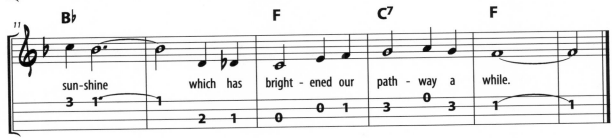

sun-shine which has bright - ened our path - way a while.

2. Come and sit by my side if you love me;
   Do not hasten to bid me adieu,
   But remember the Red River Valley,
   And the girl that has loved you so true.

3. I've been thinking a long time, my darling,
   Of the sweet words you never would say,
   Now, alas, must my fond hopes all vanish?
   For they say you are going away.

4. Won't you think of the valley you're leaving,
   Oh, how lonely and sad it will be,
   Just think of the fond heart you're breaking,
   And the grief you are causing to me.

5. From this valley they say you are going,
   When you go, may your darling go too?
   Would you leave her behind unprotected,
   When she loves no one other than you.

6. As you go to your home by the ocean,
   May you never forget those sweet hours,
   That we spent in the Red River Valley,
   And the love we exchanged ,mid the flowers.

7. I have promised you, darling, that never
   Will a word from my lips cause you pain,
   And my life, it will be yours forever,
   If you only will love me again.

8. They will bury me where you have wandered,
   Near the hills where the daffodils grow,
   When you're gone from the Red River valley,
   For I can't live without you I know.

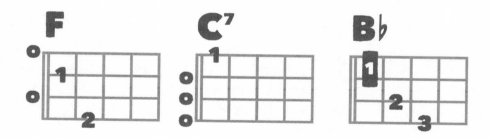

Billy Boy

2. Did she bid you to come in, Billy Boy, Billy Boy?
   Did she bid you to come in, charming Billy?
   Yes, she bade me to come in, there's a dimple in her chin.
   She's a young thing and cannot leave her mother.

3. Can she make a cherry pie, Billy Boy, Billy Boy?
   Can she make a cherry pie, charming Billy?
   She can make a cherry pie, quick as a cat can wink an eye,
   She's a young thing and cannot leave her mother.

4. Did she set for you a chair, Billy Boy, Billy Boy?
   Did she set for you a chair, charming Billy?
   Yes, she sat for me a chair, she has ringlets in her hair.
   She's a young thing and cannot leave her mother.

5. How old is she now, Billy Boy, Billy Boy?
   How old is she now, charming Billy?
   Three times six and four times seven, twenty-eight and eleven,
   She's a young thing and cannot leave her mother.

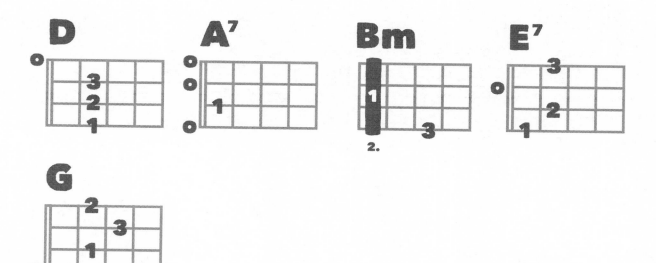

America the beautiful

2. O beautiful for pilgrim feet
   Whose stern impassioned stress
   A thoroughfare of freedom beat
   Across the wilderness!
   America! America!
   God mend thine every flaw,
   Confirm thy soul in self-control,
   Thy liberty in law!

3. O beautiful for heroes proved
   In liberating strife.
   Who more than self their country loved
   And mercy more than life!
   America! America!
   May God thy gold refine
   Till all success be nobleness
   And every gain divine!

4. O beautiful for patriot dream
   That sees beyond the years
   Thine alabaster cities gleam
   Undimmed by human tears!
   America! America!
   God shed his grace on thee
   And crown thy good with brotherhood
   From sea to shining sea!

5. O beautiful for halcyon skies,
   For amber waves of grain,
   For purple mountain majesties
   Above the enameled plain!
   America! America!
   God shed his grace on thee
   Till souls wax fair as earth and air
   And music-hearted sea!

6. O beautiful for pilgrims feet,
   Whose stem impassioned stress
   A thoroughfare for freedom beat
   Across the wilderness!
   America! America!
   God shed his grace on thee
   Till paths be wrought through wilds of thought
   By pilgrim foot and knee!

7. O beautiful for glory-tale
   Of liberating strife
   When once and twice, for man's avail
   Men lavished precious life!
   America! America!
   God shed his grace on thee
   Till selfish gain no longer stain
   The banner of the free!

8. O beautiful for patriot dream
   That sees beyond the years
   Thine alabaster cities gleam
   Undimmed by human tears!
   America! America!
   God shed his grace on thee
   Till nobler men keep once again
   Thy whiter jubilee!

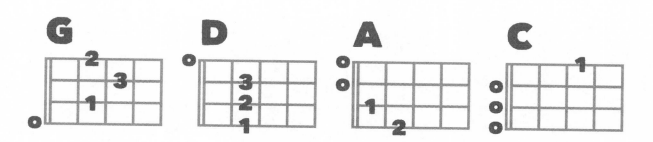

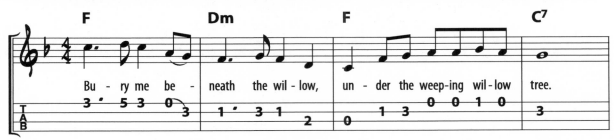

Bury me beneath the willow

Bu - ry me be - neath the wil - low, un - der the weep-ing wil - low tree.

When he finds where I am sleep - ing, may - be then he'll think of me.

2. My heart is sad I am lonely,
   For the only one I love.
   When shall I see her oh no never,
   'Til we meet in heaven above.

3. She told me that she dearly loved me.
   How could I believe it untrue,
   Until the angels softly whispered,
   She will prove untrue to you.

4. Tomorrow was to be our wedding,
   God, oh God, where can she be.
   She's out a courting with another,
   And no longer cares for me

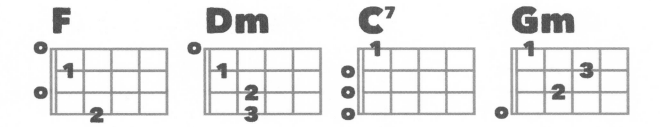

Sailor on the deep blue sea

It was on one sum-mer's eve-ning, just a-bout the hour of three, when my dar-ling start-ed to leave me, for to sail up-on the deep blue sea.

2. Oh, he promised to write me a letter,
   He said he'd write to me;
   But I've not heard from my darling
   Who is sailing on the deep blue sea.

3. Oh, my mother's dead and buried,
   My pa's forsaken me,
   And I have no one for to love me
   But the sailor on the deep blue sea.

4. Oh captain, can you tell me
   Where can my sailor be;
   Oh yes, my little maiden,
   He is drownded in the deep blue sea.

5. Farewell to friends and relations,
   It's the last you'll see of me;
   For I'm going to end my troubles
   By drowning in the deep blue sea.

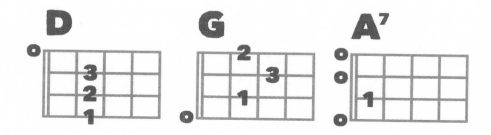

She moved through the fair

She moved through the fair

2. She stepped away from me
   And she moved through the fair
   And fondly I watched her
   Move here and move there.
   And then she made her way homeward,
   With one star awake,
   As the swan in the evening
   Moved over the lake.

3. The people were saying,
   No two e'er were wed
   But one had a sorrow
   That never was said.
   And I smiled as she passed
   With her goods and her gear,
   And that was the last
   That I saw of my dear

4. Last night she came to me,
   My dead love came in.
   So softly she came
   That her feet made no din.
   As she laid her hand on me,
   And this she did say:
   It will not be long, love,
   'Til our wedding day.

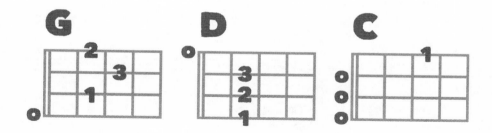

God rest ye merry, gentlemen

God rest ye merry, gentlemen

2. In Bethlehem, in Israel,
   This blessed Babe was born,
   And laid within a manger
   Upon this blessed morn,
   The which His Mother Mary
   Did nothing take in scorn:
   O tidings ...

3. From God our heavenly Father
   A blessèd angel came,
   And unto certain shepherds
   Brought tidings of the same,
   How that in Bethlehem was born
   The Son of God by name:
   O tidings ...

4. The shepherds at those tidings
   Rejoicèd much in mind,
   And left their flocks a-feeding
   In tempest, storm and wind,
   And went to Bethlehem straightway,
   This blessèd Babe to find:
   O tidings ...

5. But when to Bethlehem they came,
   Whereat this Infant lay,
   They found Him in a manger,
   Where oxen feed on hay;
   His mother Mary kneeling,
   Unto the Lord did pray:
   O tidings ...

6. Now to the Lord sing praises,
   All you within this place,
   And with true love and brotherhood
   Each other now embrace;
   This holy tide of Christmas
   All others doth deface:
   O tidings ...

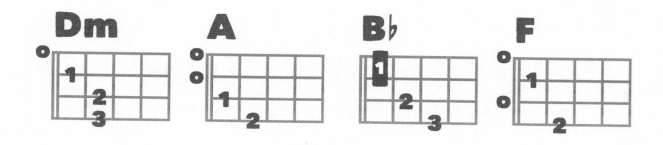

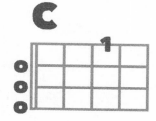

Beautiful dreamer

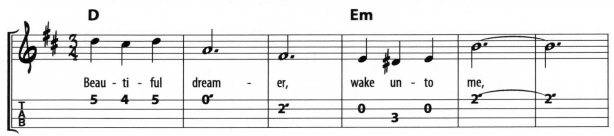

Beau - ti - ful dream - er, wake un - to me,

star - light and dew-drops are wait - ing for thee; sounds of the

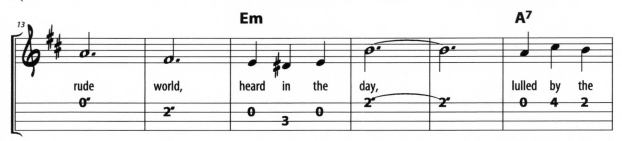

rude world, heard in the day, lulled by the

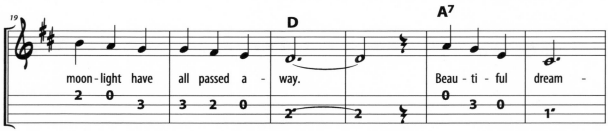

moon - light have all passed a - way. Beau - ti - ful dream -

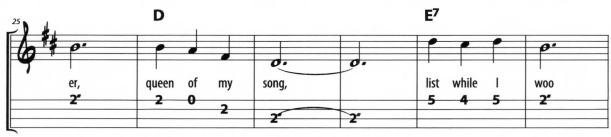

er, queen of my song, list while I woo

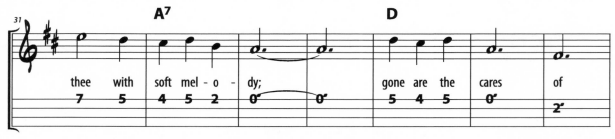

thee with soft mel - o - dy; gone are the cares of

Beautiful dreamer

life's bus - y throng, beau - ti - ful dream - er, a - wake un - to

me. Beau - ti - ful dream - er, a - wake un - to me.

2. *Beautiful dreamer, out on the sea,*
   Mermaids are chanting the wild lorelei;
   Over the streamlet vapors are borne,
   Waiting to fade at the bright coming morn.
   Beautiful dreamer, beam on my heart,
   E'en as the morn on the streamlet and sea;
   Then will all clouds of sorrow depart,
   Beautiful dreamer, awake unto me!
   Beautiful dreamer, awake unto me!

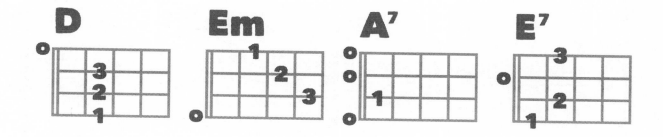

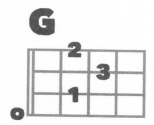

Over the river and through the woods

Over the river and through the woods

2. Over the river and through the woods,
   To have a first-rate play;
   Oh, hear the bells ring, „Ting-a-ling-ling!"
   Hurrah for Thanksgiving Day!
   Over the river and through the woods,
   Trot fast, my dapple gray!
   Spring over the ground, Like a hunting hound!
   For this is Thanksgiving Day.

3. Over the river and through the woods,
   And straight through the barnyard gate.
   We seem to go extremely slow
   It is so hard to wait!
   Over the river and through the woods,
   Now Grandmother's cap I spy!
   Hurrah for the fun! Is the pudding done?
   Hurrah for the pumpkin pie!

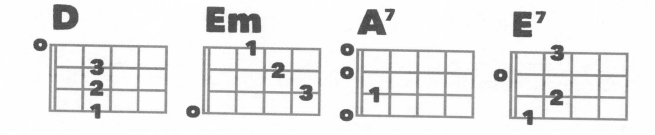

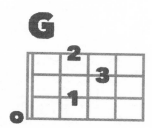

Shenandoah

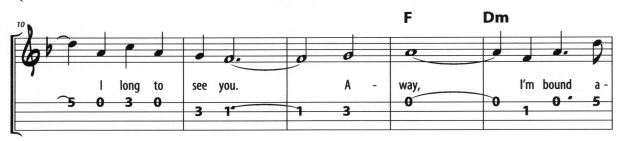

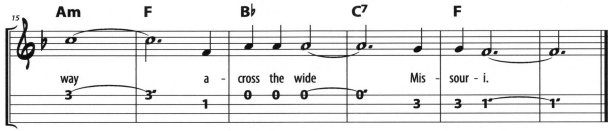

2. Oh Shenandoah,
   I love your daughter,
   Away, you rolling river.
   For her I'd cross,
   Your roaming waters,
   Away, I'm bound away,
   'Cross the wide Missouri.

3. 'Tis seven years,
   Since last I've seen you,
   Away, you rolling river.
   'Tis seven years,
   Since last I've seen you,
   Away, we're bound away,
   'Cross the wide Missouri.

F 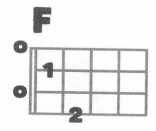 **B♭** 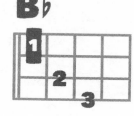 **Dm** 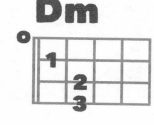 **Am**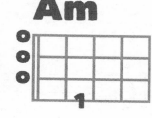

C⁷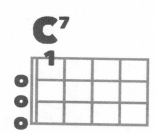

On top of Old Smokey

On top of old Smo - key, all cov - ered with snow; I lost my true lov - er a - court - ing too slow.

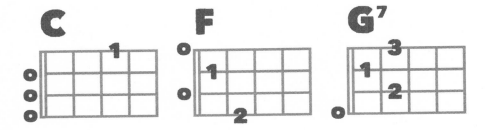

Polly put the kettle on

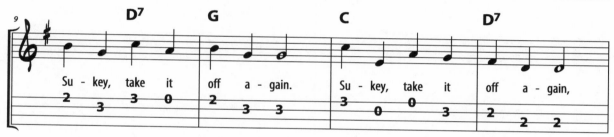

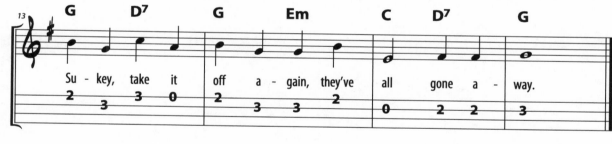

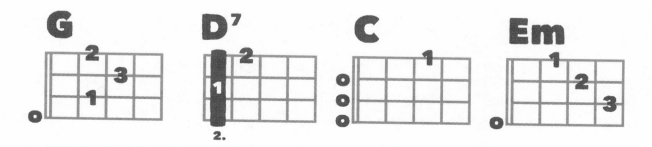

Reilly's daughter

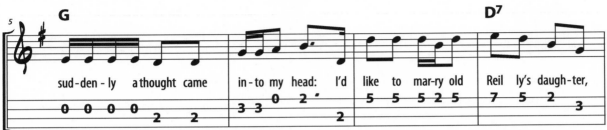

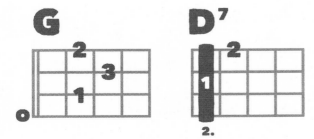

2. Reilly played on the big bass drum.
   Reilly had a mind for murder and slaughter.
   Reilly had a bright red glittering eye
   And he kept that eye on his lovely daughter.
   Giddy i-ae, Giddy i-ae ...

3. Her hair was black and her eyes were blue.
   The colonel and the major and the captain sought her.
   The sergeant and the private and the drummer boy too.
   But they never had a chance with Reilly's daughter.
   Giddy i-ae, Giddy i-ae ...

4. I got me a ring and a parson, too.
   Got me a scratch in a married quarter.
   Settled me down to a peaceful life,
   Happy as a king with Reilly's daughter.
   Giddy i-ae, Giddy i-ae ...

5. Suddenly a footstep on the stairs
   Who should it be but Reilly out for slaughter.
   With two pistols in his hands
   Looking for the man who had married his daughter.
   Giddy i-ae, Giddy i-ae ...

6. I caught O'Reilly by the hair,
   Rammed his head in a pail of water.
   Fired his pistols into the air,
   A damned sight quicker than I married his daughter.
   Giddy i-ae, Giddy i-ae ...

Cindy

2. The first I seen my Cindy she was standing in the door,
   Her shoes and stocking in her hand her feet all over the floor.

3. She took me to her parlor she cooled me with her fan,
   She said I was the prettiest thing in the shape of mortal man.

4. She kissed me and she hugged me she called me suger plum,
   She throwed her arms around me I thought my time had come.

5. Oh Cindy is a pretty girl Cindy is a peach,
   She threw her arms around my neck and hung on like a leech.

6. And if I was a sugar tree standing in the town,
   Each time my Cindy passed I'd shake some sugar down.

7. And if had a needle and thread fine as I could sew,
   I'd sew that gal to my coat tails and down the road I'd go.

8. I wish I was an apple a-hanging on a tree,
   Every time that Cindy passed she'd take a bite of me.

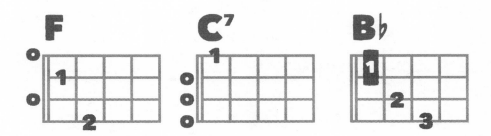

Pomp and circumstance

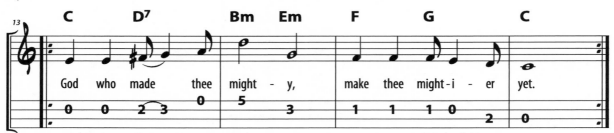

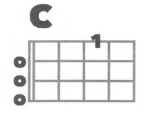

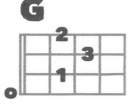

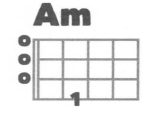

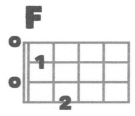

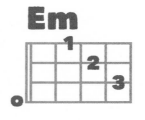

Roll in my sweet baby's arms

Ain't gon - na work on the rail - road. Ain't gon - na

work on the farm. Gon-na lay 'round this shack till the mail train comes

back, them I'll roll in my sweet ba - by's arms.

2. Now where was you last Friday night while I was lyin' in jail.
   Walkin' the streets with another man you wouldn't even go my bail
   Then I'll roll in my sweet baby's arms.

3. I know your parent don't like me they drove me away from your door.
   And my life's too bluer never to wearing more,
   Then I'll roll in my sweet baby's arms.

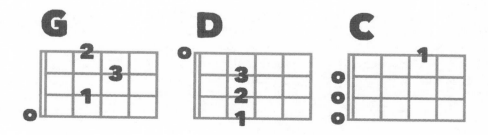

Sweet Betsy from Pike

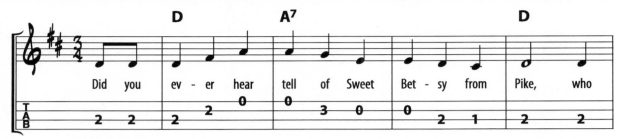

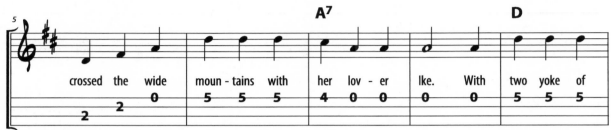

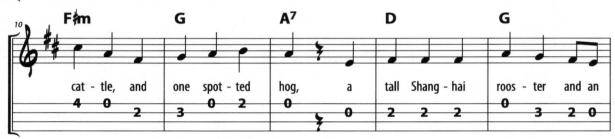

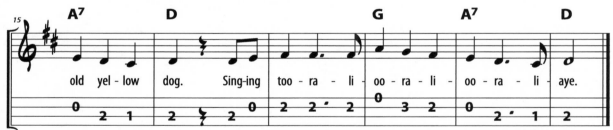

2. They swam the wide rivers and crossed the tall peaks,
   And camped on the prairie for weeks upon weeks.
   Starvation and cholera, hard work and slaughter –
   They reached California, spite of hell and high water.
   Singing too-ra-li-oo-ra-li-oo-ra-li-ay.

3. One evening quite early they camped on the Platte,
   Twas near by the road on a green shady flat.
   Betsy, sore-footed, lay down to repose –
   With wonder Ike gazed on that Pike County rose.
   Singing too-ra-li-oo-ra-li-oo-ra-li-ay.

4. The Injuns came down in a thundering horde,
   And Betsy was scared they would scalp her adored.
   So under the wagon-bed Betsy did crawl
   And she fought off the Injuns with musket and ball.
   Singing too-ra-li-oo-ra-li-oo-ra-li-ay.

5. The wagon broke down with a terrible crash,
   And out on the prairie rolled all sorts of trash.
   A few little baby-clothes, done up with care,
   Looked rather suspicious, but all on the square.
   Singing too-ra-li-oo-ra-li-oo-ra-li-ay.

6. They stopped at Salt Lake to inquire of the way,
   When Brigham declared that Sweet Betsy should stay.
   Betsy got frightened and ran like a deer,
   While Brigham stood pawing the ground like a steer.
   Singing too-ra-li-oo-ra-li-oo-ra-li-ay.

7. The alkali desert was burning and bare,
   And Isaac's soul shrank from the death that lurked there.
   "Dear old Pike County, I'll go back to you" –
   Says Betsy, "You'll go by yourself if you do!"
   Singing too-ra-li-oo-ra-li-oo-ra-li-ay.

8. They soon reached the desert, where Betsy gave out,
   And down in the sand she lay rolling about.
   Ike in great wonder looked on in surprise,
   Saying, "Betsy, get up, you'll get sand in your eyes."
   Singing too-ra-li-oo-ra-li-oo-ra-li-ay.

9. Sweet Betsy got up in a great deal of pain.
   She declared she'd go back to Pike County again.
   Ike gave a sigh, and they fondly embraced,
   And they traveled along with his arm round her waist.
   Singing too-ra-li-oo-ra-li-oo-ra-li-ay.

10. The Shanghai ran off, and the cattle all died,
    That morning the last piece of bacon was fried.
    Ike got discouraged, Betsy got mad,
    The dog drooped his tail and looked wonderfully sad.
    Singing too-ra-li-oo-ra-li-oo-ra-li-ay.

11. They suddenly stopped on a very high hill,
    With wonder looked down upon old Placerville.
    Ike said to Betsy, as he cast his eyes down,
    "Sweet Betsy, my darling, we've got to Hangtown."
    Singing too-ra-li-oo-ra-li-oo-ra-li-ay.

12. Long Ike and Sweet Betsy attended a dance.
    Ike wore a pair of his Pike County pants.
    Betsy was covered with ribbons and rings.
    Says Ike, "You're an angel, but where is your wings?"
    Singing too-ra-li-oo-ra-li-oo-ra-li-ay.

13. A miner said, "Betsy, will you dance with me?"
    "I will that, old hoss, if you don't make too free.
    Don't dance me hard, do you want to know why?
    Doggone you, I'm chock-full of strong alkali."
    Singing too-ra-li-oo-ra-li-oo-ra-li-ay.

14. This Pike County couple got married, of course,
    But Ike became jealous, and obtained a divorce.
    Betsy, well-satisfied, said with a shout,
    "Goodby, you big lummox, I'm glad you backed out!"
    Singing too-ra-li-oo-ra-li-oo-ra-li-ay.

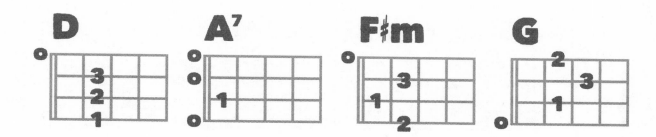

Hard times come again no more

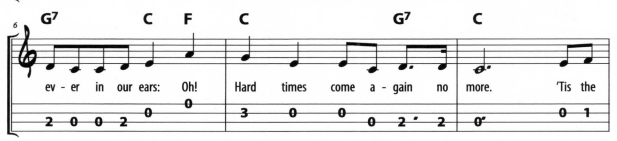

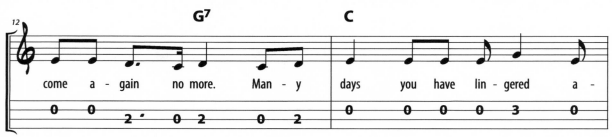

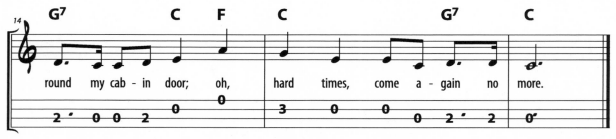

2. While we seek mirth and beauty and music light and gay,
   There are frail forms fainting at the door;
   Though their voices are silent, their pleading looks will say
   Oh! Hard times come again no more.
   'Tis the song, the sigh of the weary ...

3. There's a pale drooping maiden who toils her life away,
   With a worn heart whose better days are o'er:
   Though her voice would be merry, ,tis sighing all the day,
   Oh! Hard times come again no more.
   'Tis the song, the sigh of the weary ...

4. 'Tis a sigh that is wafted across the troubled wave,
   'Tis a wail that is heard upon the shore
   'Tis a dirge that is murmured around the lowly grave
   Oh! Hard times come again no more.
   'Tis the song, the sigh of the weary ...

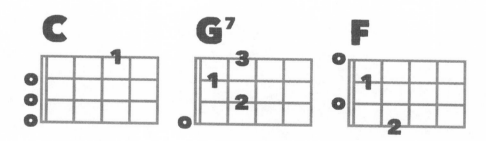

My country 'tis of thee

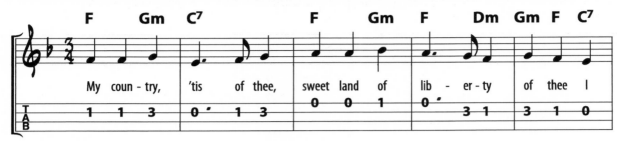

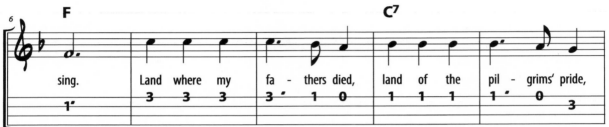

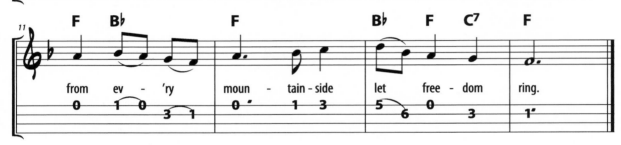

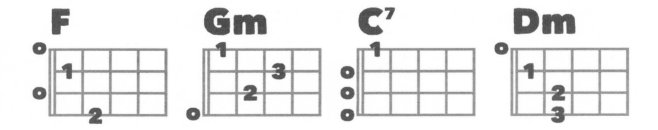

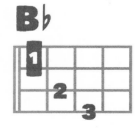

2. My native country, thee,
   Land of the noble free,
   Thy name I love;
   I love thy rocks and rills,
   Thy woods and templed hills,
   My heart with rapture thrills
   Like that above.

3. Let music swell the breeze,
   And ring from all the trees
   Sweet Freedom's song;
   Let mortal tongues awake;
   Let all that breathe partake;
   Let rocks their silence break,
   The sound prolong.

4. Our fathers' God to Thee,
   Author of Liberty,
   To thee we sing,
   Long may our land be bright
   With Freedom's holy light,
   Protect us by thy might
   Great God, our King.

5. Our glorious Land to-day,
   'Neath Education's sway,
   Soars upward still.
   Its hills of learning fair,
   Whose bounties all may share,
   Behold them everywhere
   On vale and hill!

6. Thy safeguard, Liberty,
   The school shall ever be,
   Our Nation's pride!
   No tyrant hand shall smite,
   While with encircling might
   All here are taught the Right
   With Truth allied.

7. Beneath Heaven's gracious will
   The stars of progress still
   Our course do sway;
   In unity sublime
   To broader heights we climb,
   Triumphant over Time,
   God speeds our way!

8. Grand birthright of our sires,
   Our altars and our fires
   Keep we still pure!
   Our starry flag unfurled,
   The hope of all the world,
   In peace and light impearled,
   God hold secure!

Hawaii Ponoi

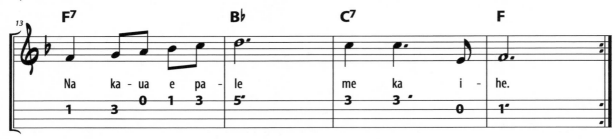

Hawaii Ponoi

1. *Hawai'i pono'ī,*
   Nānā i kou mō'ī,
   Ka lani ali'i,
   Ke ali'i.

Chorus:
   Makua lani ē,
   Kamehameha ē,
   Na kaua e pale,
   Me ka ihe.

2. *Hawai'i pono'ī,*
   Nānā i nā ali'i,
   Nā pua muli kou,
   Nā pōki'i.

3. *Hawai'i pono'ī,*
   E ka lahui ē,
   'O kāu hana nui
   E u'i ē.

1. *Hawai'i's own true sons,*
   Be loyal to your king,
   Your country's liege and lord
   The chief.

Chorus:
   Father above us all,
   Kamehameha e,
   Who guarded in the war,
   With his spear.

2. *Hawai'i's own true sons,*
   Look to your chiefs,
   The children after you,
   The young.

3. *Hawai'i's own true sons,*
   People of loyal heart,
   The only duty lies
   List and abide.

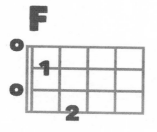
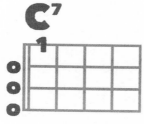
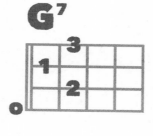
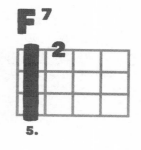

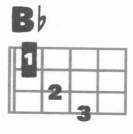

Away in a manger

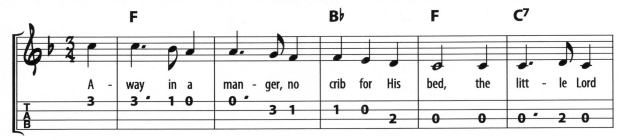

A - way in a man - ger, no crib for His bed, the litt - le Lord

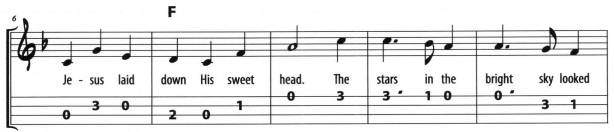

Je - sus laid down His sweet head. The stars in the bright sky looked

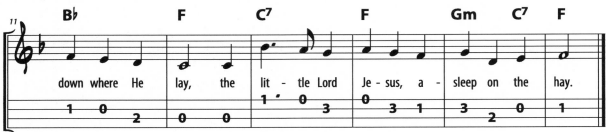

down where He lay, the lit - tle Lord Jesus, a - sleep on the hay.

2. *The cattle are lowing*
   The poor Baby wakes.
   But little Lord Jesus
   No crying He makes.
   I love Thee, Lord Jesus,
   Look down from the sky
   And stay by my side,
   'Til morning is nigh.

3. *Be near me, Lord Jesus,*
   I ask Thee to stay.
   Close by me forever
   And love me I pray.
   Bless all the dear children
   In Thy tender care
   And take us to heaven
   To live with Thee there.

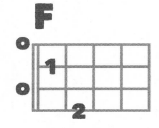
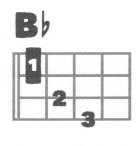
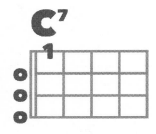
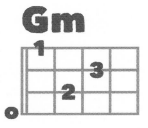

Sakura (Cherry blossoms)

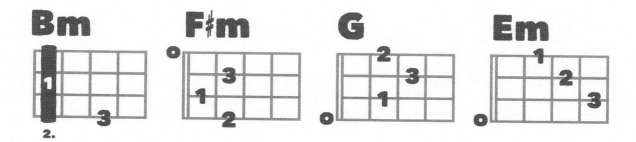

Poor Paddy works on the railroad

Poor Paddy works on the railroad

2. In eighteen hundred and forty-two
   I didn't know what I should do.
   I didn't know what I should do,
   To work upon the railway, the railway,
   I'm weary of the railway,
   Poor Paddy works on the railway.

3. In eighteen hundred and forty-three
   I sailed away across the sea.
   I sailed away across the sea,
   To work upon the railway, the railway,
   I'm weary of the railway,
   Poor Paddy works on the railway

4. In eighteen hundred and forty-four
   I landed on Columbia's shore.
   I landed on Columbia's shore,
   To work upon the railway, the railway.
   I'm weary of the railway
   Poor Paddy works on the railway.

5. In eighteen hundred and forty-five
   When Daniel O'Connell he was alive.
   When Daniel O'Connell he was alive
   To work upon the railway, the railway.
   I'm weary of the railway
   Poor Paddy works on the railway.

6. In eighteen hundred and forty-six
   I made my trade to carrying bricks.
   I made my trade to carrying bricks
   For working on the railway.
   I'm weary of the railway
   Poor Paddy works on the railway.

7. In eighteen hundred and forty-seven
   Poor Paddy was thinking of going to Heaven.
   Poor Paddy was thinking of going to Heaven
   To work upon the railway, the railway.
   I'm weary of the railway
   Poor Paddy works on the railway.

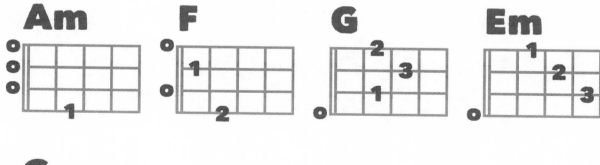

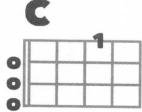

Softly and tenderly

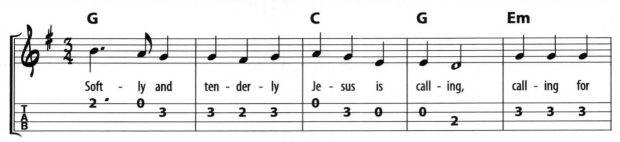

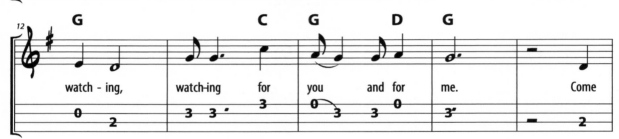

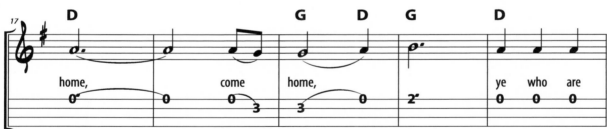

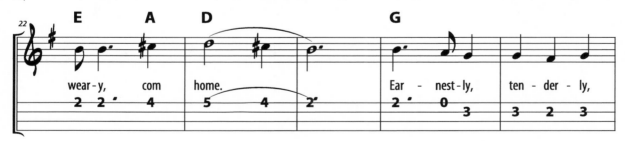

Softly and tenderly

2. Why should we tarry when Jesus is pleading,
   Pleading for you and for me.
   Why should we linger and heed not His mercies,
   Mercies for you and for me.

3. Time is now fleeting, the moments are passing,
   Passing for you and for me.
   Shadows are gathering, death's night is coming,
   Coming for you and for me.

4. O for the wonderful love He has promised,
   Promised for you and for me!
   Though we have sinned, He has mercy and pardon,
   Pardon for you and for me.

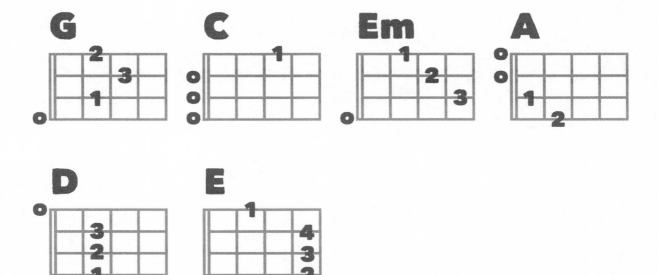

The first Noel

2. They looked up and saw a star
   Shining in the east beyond them far,
   And to the earth it gave great light,
   And so it continued both day and night.

3. And by the light of that same star
   Three wise men came from country far;
   To seek for a king was their intent,
   And to follow the star wherever it went.

4. This star drew nigh to the northwest,
   O'er Bethlehem it took it rest,
   And there it did both stop and stay
   Right over the place where Jesus lay.

5. Then entered in those wise men three
   Full reverently upon their knee,
   and offered there in his presence
   Their gold, and myrrh, and frankincense.

6. Then let us all with one accord
   Sing praises to our heavenly Lord;
   That hath made heaven and earth of naught,
   And with his blood mankind hath bought.

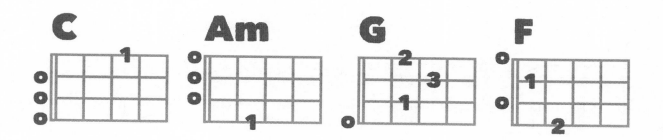

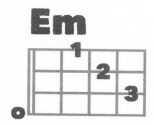

The star spangled banner

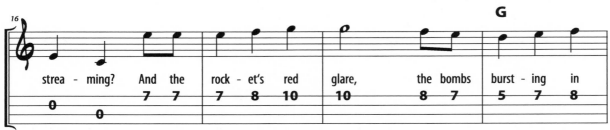

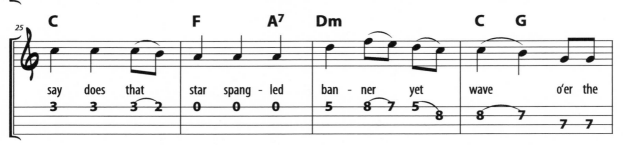

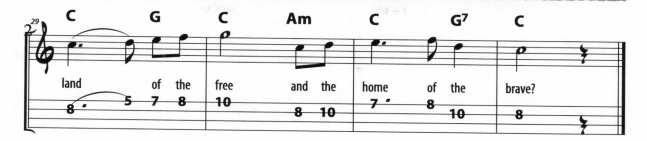

The star spangled banner

2. On the shore, dimly seen through the mists of the deep,
   Where the foe's haughty host in dread silence reposes,
   What is that which the breeze, o'er the towering steep,
   As it fitfully blows, half conceals, half discloses?
   Now it catches the gleam of the morning's first beam,
   In full glory reflected now shines in the stream:
   ,Tis the star-spangled banner! Oh long may it wave
   O'er the land of the free and the home of the brave!

3. And where is that band who so vauntingly swore
   That the havoc of war and the battle's confusion,
   A home and a country should leave us no more!
   Their blood has washed out their foul footsteps' pollution.
   No refuge could save the hireling and slave
   From the terror of flight, or the gloom of the grave:
   And the star-spangled banner in triumph doth wave
   O'er the land of the free and the home of the brave!

4. Oh! thus be it ever, when freemen shall stand
   Between their loved home and the war's desolation!
   Blest with victory and peace, may the heav'n rescued land
   Praise the Power that hath made and preserved us a nation.
   Then conquer we must, when our cause it is just,
   And this be our motto: „In God is our trust."
   And the star-spangled banner in triumph shall wave
   O'er the land of the free and the home of the brave!

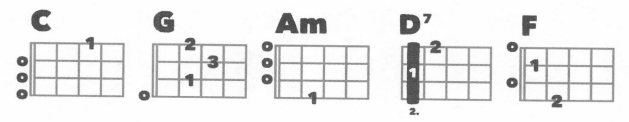

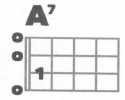

The Minstrel Boy

2. The Minstrel fell! But the foeman's chain
   Could not bring his proud soul under;
   The harp he loved ne'er spoke again,
   For he tore its chords asunder;
   And said „No chains shall sully thee,
   Thou soul of love and bravery!
   Thy songs were made for the pure and free
   They shall never sound in slavery!"

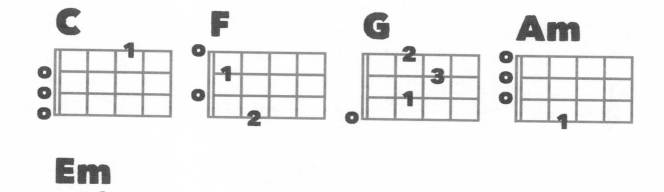

Silent night

2. Silent night, Holy night!
   Son of God, love's pure light.
   Radiant beams from thy holy face.
   With the dawn of redeeming grace,
   Jesus, Lord at thy birth,
   Jesus, Lord at thy birth.

3. Silent night, Holy night!
   Shepherds quake at the sight.
   Glories stream from heaven above.
   Heavenly, hosts sing Hallelujah,
   Christ the Savior is born,
   Christ the Savior is born.

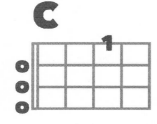
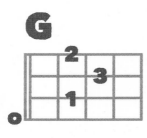
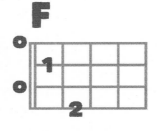
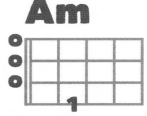

Up on the housetop

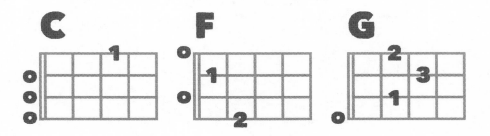

C   F   G

89

Horizontal lines represent the strings of the Ukulele, vertical lines the frets.

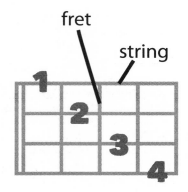

The finger of the fretting hand are numbered 1-4:
1 = Index finger
2 = Middle finger
3 = Ringfinger
4 = Little finger (pinky)

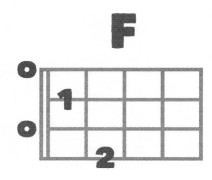

The chord symbol is given above the chord

Open strings are indicated by an "0" to the left of the diagram, mutes strings (strings that are not played or damped) by an "x".

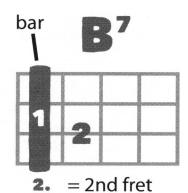

2. = 2nd fret

Fretboard positions are indicated below the chord. If a chord is to be played as a so-called bar chord (i.e. fretting more than one string with the same finger) this is indicated by a black bar. The number inside the bar indicates the recommended fretting finger.

Tuning the Ukulele

The strings of the Ukulele are numbered 1-4 (starting with the one next to the floor).

1st string = A
2nd string = E
3rd string = C
4th string = G

In contrast to most other string instruments, the strings of the Ukulele are tuned in what is called a reentrant tuning (meaning the lowest tuned string of the instrument is not the bottom string). This can make tuning the instrument slightly confusing, especially for beginners.
There are lots of ways to tune your Ukulele, one of which is shown below in graphical form.

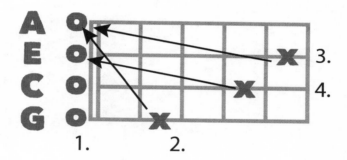

This reads as follows:

1. First tune the G string using a reference tone from another Instrument (Ilke a piano) or a tuner.
2. Fret the G string at the 2. fret. Play and compare to the open (not fretted) A string. Tune the A string until both pitches match exactly.
3. Fret the E string at the 5. Fret. Play and compare to the open A string. Tune the E string until both pitches match.
4. Finally, fret the C string at the 4. Fret. Play and compare to the E string.

Tune the E string until both pitches match.

PS. Of course, using an (electronic) tuner is a great way to tune tour Ukulele, too.

Strumming patterns

The following is a selection of basic strumming pattern which you can use for song accompaniment. These are just for starters - you'll soon use other, more elaborate pattern or invent your own. Feel free to use a pick or your finger(s) for strumming - basically whatever feels best.

Here's how they're read:

- The horizontal lines represent the strings of your Ukulele.
  Downstroke (strumming in the direction of the floor): arrow upward
  Upstroke: arrow downward.
- The length of the arrows indicates which strings to strum.
- Each of these pattern shows a whole measure.

For song accompaniment you can choose (and also combine) whatever pattern feels best to you, but keep in mind to match the pattern's time to the time of the song, e.g. for a song in 4/4 time only use strumming patterns in 4/4 time.
Songs in 2/2 time can be played using strumming patterns in 4/4 time.

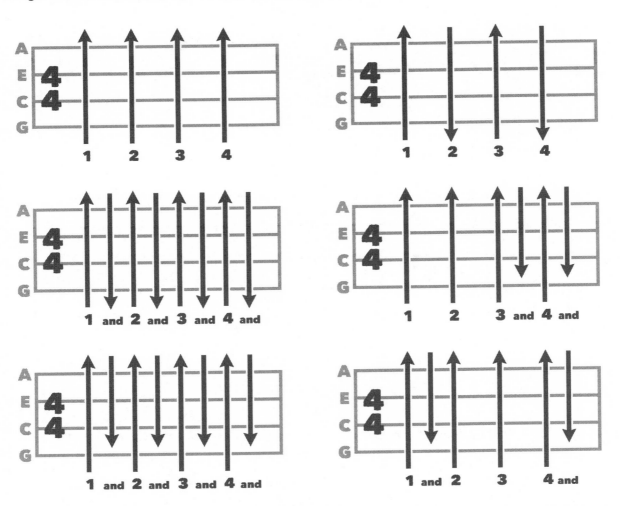

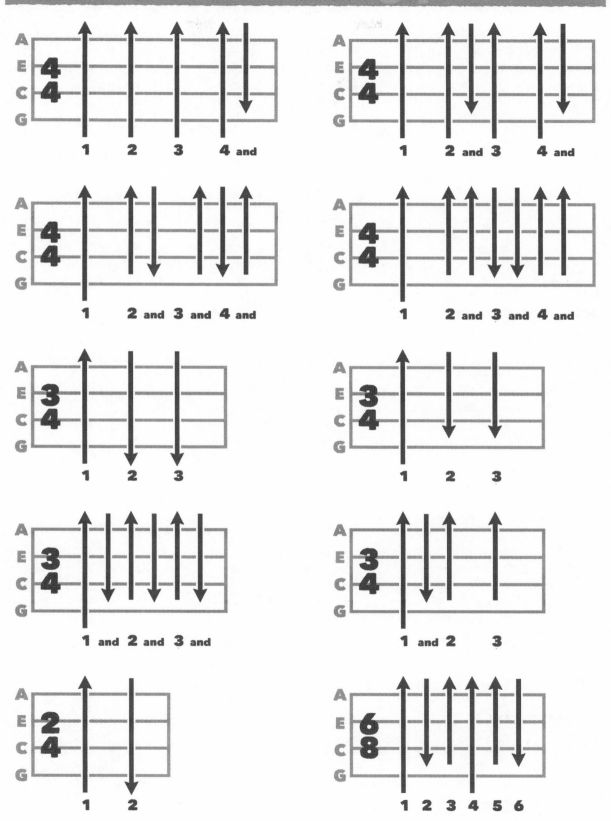

Picking patterns

A lot of songs sound particularly good when played using a picking pattern. Here's the basic idea: instead of picking all the notes of a chord simultaneously with you finger(s) or a pick, you play them successively, one after the other. Picking patterns are commonly used for longer musical sections (or even whole songs) and adapted to the chord changes if necessary. Here's an example, using the G major chord:

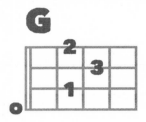

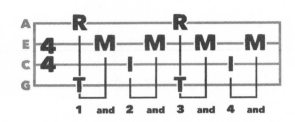

T = thumb
I = Index finger
M = Middle finger
R = ring finger

As in tablature, horizontal lines represent the strings of your Ukulele. The time signature is notated at the beginning of the pattern as a fraction (here: 4/4; this is a pattern for songs in 4/4 time). The letters T, I, M and R indicate the fingers of the picking hand. Below the pattern I've notated how to count it. Here's a step-by-step explanation of the above example:
- on the first beat ("1") thumb and ring finger simultaneously pick the G string and the A string.
- on the second half of the first beat ("1and") the middle finger picks the E string.
- on the second beat ("2") the index finger picks the C string.
- on the second half of the second beat ("2and") the middle finger picks the E string once again.
This pattern is repeated for the second half of the bar (this isn't always the case).

There are a few basic things to keep in mind when using picking patterns:
Obviously, the pattern's time signature has to match that of the song. In some cases, the pattern has to be adapted to a certain chord or a chord change, but most of the time you can use the following simple rule:
• pick the G string with your thumb,
• the C string with your index finger,
• the E string with your middle finger and
• the A string with your ring finger.

One of the best ways to practise picking patterns is to play them on open strings until the movement of your fingers becomes second nature – practicing this way ensures you'll be able to concentrate on more important things when it's time to play the song.
When the picking pattern has been "automized" to a certain degree it's time to add chords and chord changes. Take your time because nothing sounds worse than a "stuttering" picking pattern interfering with a smooth chord change.
On the following pages you'll find some basic picking patterns to choose from. Of course, this is just a small selection from the multitude of possible patterns, meant to whet your appetite – you'll soon find varying patterns and inventing new ones of your own can be lots of fun!

For a start, you may want to try:
• Combining different picking patterns
  (e. g. one for the verse and one for the chorus).
• Combining picking patterns with strumming patterns.
• Mixing picking patterns with melody lines and damping techniques.
• Playing some of your favorites "backwards".

Sometimes you'll encounter indications in Spanish:
P (pulgar) = thumb
I (indice) = index finger
M (medio) = middle finger
A (anular) = ring finger

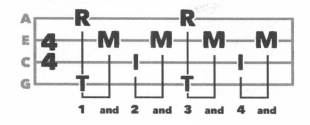

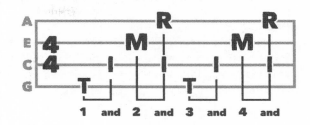

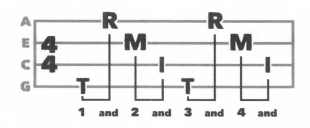

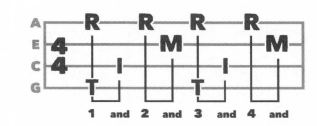

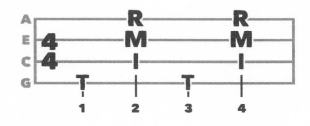

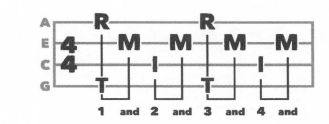

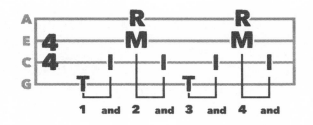

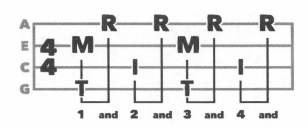

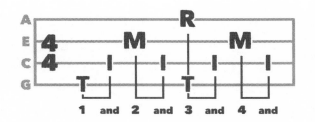

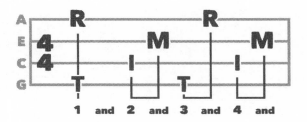

Basic chords

On the following pages I've compiled the chords used in this book. I've also included some chords you'll probably encounter in other books. Naturally, this chord collection is far from complete – there are literally thousands of Ukulele chords (some common, some pretty obscure). If you want to expand your chord repertoire (or simply look up a chord you don't know), a chord chart is always a wise investment, and of course you can find almost any Ukulele chord on the internet.

Depending on the musical context, some chords may have more than one name:

$$C\sharp = D\flat, \quad D\sharp = E\flat, \quad F\sharp = G\flat, \quad G\sharp = A\flat \quad \text{und} \quad A\sharp = B\flat$$

For Ukulele players this simply means: C♯ and D♭ are played the same and they sound the same. If, for example, you happen to stumble upon a G♯m (G sharp minor) chord, don't worry: just play A♭m.

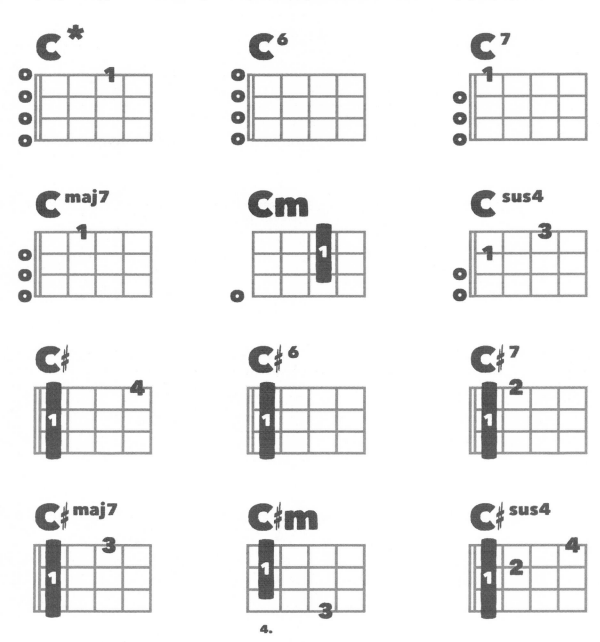

* = Alternate fingering for this chord: ring finger (3)

D

D⁶

2.

D⁷

2.

Dᵐᵃʲ⁷

2.

Dm

Dˢᵘˢ⁴

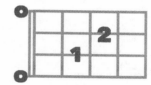

E♭

E♭⁶

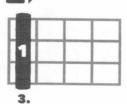

3.

E♭⁷

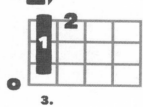

3.

E♭ᵐᵃʲ⁷

3.

E♭m

E♭⁷/ˢᵘˢ⁴

3.

E

E⁶

E⁷

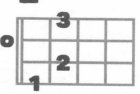

Basic chords

E^{maj7}

Em
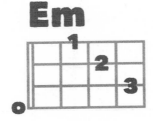

E^{sus4}
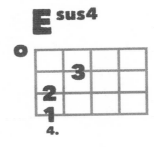

F
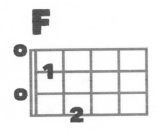

F⁶
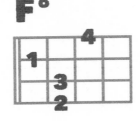

F⁷
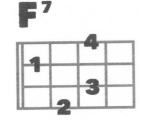

F^{maj7}
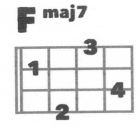

Fm
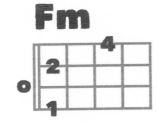

F^{sus4}
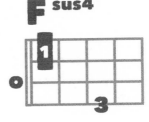

F♯ *
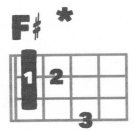

F♯⁶
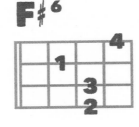

F♯⁷
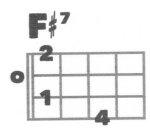

F♯^{maj7}

F♯**m**
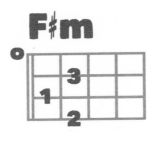

F♯^{sus4}

* = This chord can also be played as a full bar chord.

G

G⁶

G⁷

Gᵐᵃʲ⁷
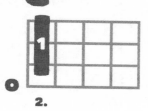

2.

Gm

Gˢᵘˢ⁴
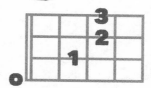

A♭

A♭⁶

A♭⁷

A♭ᵐᵃʲ⁷

A♭m
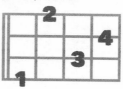

A♭ˢᵘˢ⁴
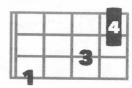

A
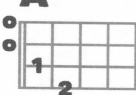

A⁶

A⁷

Basic chords

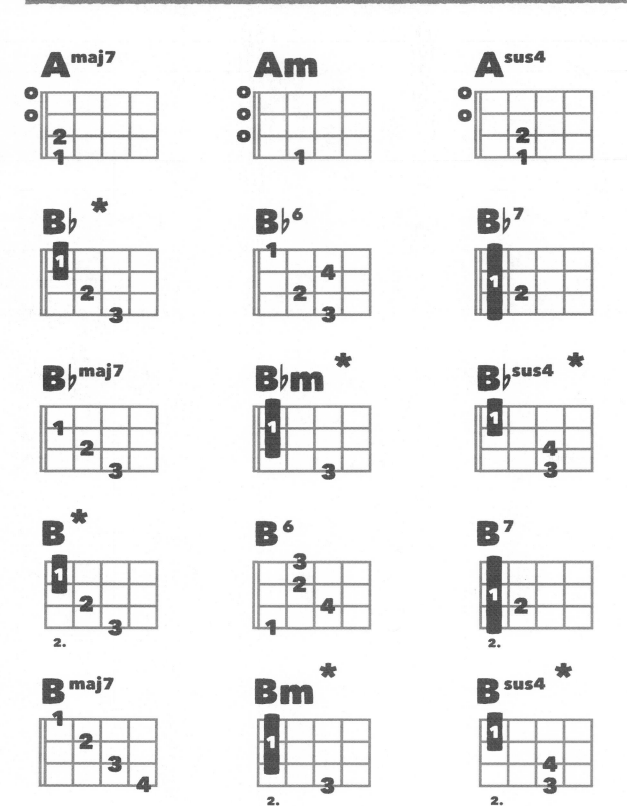

* = These chords can also be played as full bar chords.

Ukulele Songbooks
by Thomas Balinger

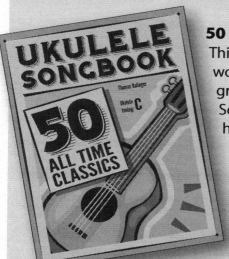

50 All time classics

This book features 50 songs known and loved the world over, arranged for Ukulele. From „Amazing grace" and „Camptown races" to Banks of the Ohio" or Scarborough fair": songs every Ukulele player simply has to know!

50 All time classics, Vol. II

The follow-up to the successful "Ukulele Classics" songbook, this handy collection contains another 50 great songs, arranged for easy Ukulele in C (G-C-E-A).

Children's Songs

Whether you're a nursery teacher, a loving parent or just love making music for children: on these pages, you'll find children's songs loved all around the world in easy-to-play arrangements for Ukulele.

Best of Gospel

Who doesn't know famous Gospel songs like "When the saints go marchin' in" or "Down by the riverside"? But hold on – there's more to Gospel than just the "hits"!

Made in the USA
Lexington, KY
15 December 2017